CW01645977

MAYER SMITH

Hidden Fortune, True Love

First edition

This book was professionally typeset on Reedsy.
Find out more at reedsy.com

Contents

One

A Masked Beginning

Julian Hart stood at the window of his penthouse, gazing out at the sprawling cityscape below. The city glittered in the late afternoon sun, a web of streets and towering buildings stretching as far as the eye could see. It was a beautiful view, one that most people would envy. Yet, for Julian, it felt hollow, as though the world outside was nothing more than a distant reflection of the life he had carefully built—a life that had started to feel like a gilded cage.

The luxury of his apartment, the designer clothes that filled his closet, the cars that lined his private garage—it all meant nothing to him now. He had it all, yet he felt utterly alone. People had always been drawn to him, but not for who he was. They were drawn to his wealth, his status, his success. Julian had learned long ago that money was the easiest way to make people love you—or at least pretend to. But it wasn't real. None of it was real.

A knock on the door interrupted his thoughts. Julian turned, his heart rate quickening slightly, not because he was startled, but because he knew exactly who it was. It was his assistant, Greg, come to remind him of his obligations.

"Come in," Julian called, his voice flat.

Greg entered, his expression a mix of professionalism and concern. "Mr. Hart, your 3:00 meeting is about to start. Are you ready?"

Julian nodded absently, his mind still somewhere else. "I'll be down in a moment."

Greg hesitated. "Is everything okay, sir? You seem… distracted."

Julian didn't respond immediately. Instead, he walked to the bar and poured himself a glass of whiskey. He needed the burn to clear his thoughts. After a long sip, he turned to Greg, meeting his gaze with a look that was as tired as it was decisive.

"Greg, have you ever wondered if it's all worth it? The money, the fame, the power… all of it?"

Greg's brow furrowed, but he kept his composure. "Of course, Mr. Hart. But you've earned everything you have. Most people would give anything to be in your position."

Julian set the glass down with a soft clink. "That's the problem,

Greg. Everyone wants what I have, but no one cares who I am. They just want my money. They don't love me, they love the idea of me."

Greg opened his mouth to speak, but Julian cut him off. "I've been thinking about it for a while. I want to try something different."

Greg blinked in confusion. "Different? Sir, with all due respect, you've built an empire. You're the top of the top. What exactly do you mean by 'different'?"

Julian walked to the window again, his back to Greg. "I'm going to step out of this world. I want to see if anyone can love me for who I am, not what I have."

"Step out?" Greg repeated, his voice rising with disbelief. "But, sir, that's impossible! You can't just throw everything away! People depend on you. Your business—"

"I'll handle it," Julian interrupted, his voice cold. "I'm going to live like a normal person for once. A regular guy, with no money, no influence, no name. I'll see if anyone cares about me when I have nothing to offer."

Greg stood in stunned silence for a long moment before he finally spoke, his voice hesitant. "And... you plan to do this how, exactly?"

Julian turned and faced him, a shadow of a smile on his lips. "I'm going to disappear. I'll take on a new identity, a new life.

No one will know who I am."

Greg stared at him, trying to comprehend what he was hearing. "Sir, are you... serious?"

"I've never been more serious," Julian replied, his gaze unwavering.

—-

The days that followed were a blur of preparation and careful planning. Julian took great pains to create his new persona, ensuring that no trace of his past life remained. He shaved his beard and cut his hair, adopting a scruffy, unkempt look. His sharp, tailored suits were replaced with worn jeans and a simple hoodie. He even picked up a fake ID from an old contact in the city, someone who owed him a favor from years ago. The ID gave him a new name, one that wasn't tied to anything—just another man in a city full of men.

Once everything was in place, Julian left his penthouse behind, the place that had been his sanctuary for so long now feeling like a prison. He boarded a plane to a small, quiet town on the outskirts of the city. It wasn't far, but it was enough to put distance between him and his past life. In this new place, he could be just another face in the crowd.

As he stepped off the plane, a sense of exhilaration rushed through him, mingled with a quiet anxiety. This was it. There would be no turning back.

—-

Julian settled into a small apartment in the town, its peeling paint and outdated furniture a far cry from the sleek, modern spaces he was used to. It was a humble existence, but it felt... freeing. He didn't have to worry about board meetings, gala events, or people fawning over him for his money. Here, he was just another guy trying to get by.

But as the days passed, Julian began to realize something unsettling. It wasn't just the lack of luxury that he missed. It was the emptiness that came with living without his identity. Without the recognition of who he was, Julian felt a deep, gnawing sense of loneliness. The relationships he had before were shallow, yes, but they had been relationships nonetheless. Now, no one cared. No one even looked at him twice.

He spent his days working odd jobs—mostly in cafes and bookstores—and his nights were spent alone in his small apartment. He found himself drifting from one place to the next, watching people around him form connections, and he wondered if he could ever truly belong in this world.

But everything changed when he met her.

It happened on a rainy afternoon when Julian was sitting at the counter of a local coffee shop, nursing a cup of black coffee. His eyes wandered over the faces of the people around him, each of them lost in their own lives, oblivious to the quiet man in the corner. That was when she walked in.

Clara.

She entered the café with an air of grace that immediately drew Julian's attention. Her hair was tied back in a messy bun, and she wore a faded jean jacket over a simple t-shirt. She was nothing special, nothing like the glamorous women Julian was used to. Yet, there was something about her—something that made Julian's heart beat faster.

She ordered a coffee and glanced around, looking for a place to sit. Her eyes met his for just a second, and she smiled politely before taking a seat at the table across from him. Julian couldn't stop staring. There was something magnetic about her—a warmth that he hadn't felt in years.

As the minutes passed, he found himself wondering if she could be the one. The one person who might care about him for who he was, not what he had. But he quickly shook the thought away. He was just a nobody now. Just another guy.

But Clara, it seemed, wasn't so quick to judge.

She looked up again, this time holding his gaze a little longer. Then, with a boldness that surprised him, she spoke.

"Is this seat taken?"

Julian's heart skipped a beat. "Uh... no," he stammered, "It's free."

She smiled and sat down. And just like that, Julian's world

began to shift.

Two

The First Encounter

The small café was a cozy haven in the middle of the bustling town. The sound of rain tapping against the windows and the soft hum of conversations created a sense of warmth that Julian hadn't felt in a long time. His fingers nervously wrapped around his coffee cup as he watched Clara settle into the seat across from him, her casual grace catching his attention in a way he couldn't quite explain.

Julian had been careful to keep his distance from people, to fade into the background, but there was something about Clara that drew him in. Her smile, though brief, seemed genuine, and her demeanor was calm and unassuming. Unlike the women he was used to—the ones who were always dressed to impress, always on the lookout for something—Clara seemed different. She wasn't looking for attention; she was simply living in the moment, savoring her coffee, and reading her book.

A strange feeling of discomfort mixed with fascination churned in his chest. He had spent so long living a life where every interaction was calculated, where every conversation was about appearances and status. But with Clara, he didn't feel the need to be anything more than what he was—just a man sitting at a café, trying to get through the day.

For a long moment, neither of them spoke. Julian couldn't help but watch her as she read, the faint smile on her lips betraying her enjoyment of the words in front of her. He knew nothing about her, yet he felt an inexplicable connection—a pull that he hadn't experienced before. It was a dangerous feeling, one that he had buried beneath layers of wealth and power for years. But here, in this small café, with nothing more than a cup of coffee between them, that feeling surged back, threatening to unravel the facade he had worked so hard to create.

Finally, Clara looked up from her book, her eyes meeting his with an intensity that made his breath catch. She didn't look away immediately, as most people would. Instead, she held his gaze, and for the first time in what felt like ages, Julian felt seen—not for his money, not for his status, but for who he was in that moment. The real, raw man behind the mask he wore.

"Do you mind if I ask you something?" Clara's voice was soft, yet her words carried an edge of curiosity.

Julian blinked, caught off guard by her directness. He cleared his throat before responding, trying to sound casual, though inside he felt the weight of the moment.

"Go ahead," he said, his voice surprisingly steady.

She hesitated for just a moment before leaning forward, her hands folded neatly on the table. "What's your story? I mean, everyone has one, right? Why are you here, sitting alone, in the middle of the afternoon, just... staring out the window?"

Julian's stomach tightened. The question was innocent enough, but the way she asked it felt like a challenge. A challenge he wasn't sure he was ready to face. For the first time, he realized that he didn't have an answer ready. He had spent so many years crafting his public persona, rehearsing the answers to the questions he knew people would ask him, but now, faced with Clara's genuine curiosity, he had no words.

"I... I'm just passing through," he said, his voice sounding almost too casual, too rehearsed. He tried to make it sound convincing, but even he could tell it didn't sit right.

Clara tilted her head slightly, studying him with a thoughtful expression. "Passing through? You don't look like a 'passing through' kind of guy."

Julian stiffened, his mind racing. She wasn't buying it. Of course, she wouldn't. He looked out of place in this small town, a man out of sync with his surroundings. His clothes, though modest compared to what he used to wear, still carried the remnants of his former life—clean, pressed, too new for a man trying to blend in with the locals. His hands, though calloused from the menial work he had been doing, still had an elegant grace to them, an unconscious reminder of who he had once been.

"I guess I'm not," he said, unable to hide the slight edge in his voice. "But I'm here now. And that's what matters."

Clara seemed to accept the answer, though her eyes lingered on him for a moment longer. There was something in her gaze—something sharp and perceptive—that made Julian uncomfortable. It was as if she could see through the layers he had so carefully built around himself.

"So," she continued, her voice lighter now, "what's your name?"

Julian's mind froze. He hadn't expected this. His real name—Julian Hart—was tied to everything he had left behind. To say it would be to risk exposing the lie he was living, the false persona he had constructed. The name he had been given, the life he had created—everything would crumble.

He cleared his throat again, his thoughts scrambling. "I'm…Jack. Just Jack."

Clara smiled, though there was a flicker of uncertainty in her eyes. "Nice to meet you, Jack."

There it was again—her warmth, her openness. She wasn't judging him. She wasn't prying for some hidden agenda. She was just curious. And that curiosity, that genuine interest in who he was beneath the surface, sent a strange flutter of hope through him. Maybe—just maybe—this wasn't all a mistake. Maybe he could find what he was looking for here, in this quiet corner of the world, where no one knew who he really was.

"So," Clara said, breaking the silence once more, "what do you do, Jack?"

The question caught him off guard, and he struggled to keep his face neutral. What did he do? A part of him wanted to tell her the truth—that he was a man who had it all, a man who had more money than he could ever spend. But another part of him recoiled at the thought. Would she still want to talk to him if she knew? Would she even care?

"I'm... just getting by," he said, offering a shrug. "Working odd jobs. Nothing fancy."

Clara's brow furrowed slightly, but she didn't press him for more. "I see. Well, you've got the look of someone who's just... trying to find their place in the world. I can respect that."

Julian felt a knot tighten in his chest. Was she on to him? Did she know more than she was letting on? He couldn't shake the feeling that Clara was the type of person who saw through people—the type who could sense when something wasn't quite right.

But then again, maybe he was just being paranoid. He had spent so many years in a world of deception and manipulation that he had forgotten how to trust. He had forgotten what it was like to have a simple, honest conversation.

"Well, maybe you're right," he said finally, a reluctant smile tugging at his lips. "I'm definitely still figuring things out."

Clara smiled back, her eyes softening. "Aren't we all?"

And in that moment, Julian realized something. For the first time in a long time, he wasn't afraid. He wasn't afraid of being vulnerable, of showing a part of himself that no one had ever seen before. Clara had a way of making him feel... human again. And though the fear of being exposed still lingered in the back of his mind, he couldn't deny the pull he felt toward her.

She wasn't interested in his wealth. She wasn't interested in his power. She was just interested in him. And that, more than anything, scared him more than he was willing to admit.

But for now, he would take it. He would take this moment, this conversation, this feeling. Because something told him that it wouldn't last forever.

Three

A Glimpse into the Past

The rain had stopped, leaving the air crisp and cool, the streets shimmering with the remnants of a storm that had passed through. Julian stood at the edge of the town's modest park, his hands stuffed in the pockets of his worn jacket. He hadn't planned to come here, but somehow, his feet had carried him to this quiet place. The sound of children's laughter filled the air as they played near the swings, their carefree joy a stark contrast to the weight that Julian felt pressing down on him.

As he watched them, memories began to resurface—memories he had buried deep inside, the kind that always seemed to creep back when he least expected it. His eyes drifted to the towering trees lining the park, their branches swaying gently in the breeze. There was a certain sadness in their movement, as if they, too, understood the burden he carried.

For a moment, Julian closed his eyes, allowing the memories to wash over him. They were memories he hadn't visited in years, memories from a time when he was someone else—someone different, before the money, before the fame.

—-

It was a warm summer day, and Julian was just a boy of ten, playing in the backyard of his family's sprawling estate. The grass beneath him was soft, the scent of freshly mowed lawns mingling with the sweet smell of blooming flowers. His father had promised to spend the afternoon with him, teaching him how to throw a football, but Julian had learned by now not to expect too much.

He glanced up at the large mansion that loomed over them, its windows gleaming with the light of the afternoon sun. It was beautiful, a symbol of the wealth and success his father had worked so hard to achieve. But as he looked at the house, Julian couldn't help but feel small. He was always small in his father's eyes—just a boy who would never quite measure up to the expectations that had been set for him.

"Julian!" His father's voice cut through the air, sharp and commanding. "Get your head in the game."

Julian blinked, snapping out of his thoughts. He had been so lost in the past that he hadn't even noticed the ball flying toward him. He fumbled with it, his hands clumsy and uncertain. The ball bounced off his chest and hit the ground with a dull thud.

His father groaned, rubbing his temples in frustration. "You need to focus! You'll never be successful if you don't take things seriously."

The words stung, as they always did. Julian wanted to impress his father, to prove that he was worthy of the legacy that had been passed down to him. But no matter how hard he tried, it was never enough. His father's standards were impossibly high, and Julian's every mistake seemed to be magnified in his eyes.

"Sorry, Dad," Julian mumbled, his voice barely a whisper.

His father didn't answer. Instead, he turned and walked back toward the house, leaving Julian standing in the yard, feeling small and insignificant once again. He was used to it by now. His father's love had always felt conditional, a prize that could only be earned through achievement, through success. And Julian wasn't sure he would ever be able to win it.

—-

The memory faded as quickly as it had come, leaving Julian with a bitter taste in his mouth. He had tried for years to earn his father's approval, to make him proud, but it was always a futile effort. No matter how much he achieved, it was never enough. The emptiness that had followed him into adulthood had its roots in those early years—those moments when he realized that love, in his world, was something that had to be bought, something that had to be earned.

He opened his eyes, staring at the park in front of him as the memories continued to surface. The sound of laughter from the children echoed in his ears, reminding him of the joy he had never been able to experience. His father had taught him the value of success, but had never shown him the value of love. And it was that love—genuine, untainted—that Julian had been seeking ever since.

—-

Julian's thoughts drifted to his mother. Unlike his father, she had always been warm and affectionate, but her love came with its own set of complications. She had been a beautiful woman, always the picture of grace and poise. But beneath her calm exterior, there was an air of sadness that Julian had never fully understood.

He could still remember the way she would look at him when he was a child, her eyes filled with a longing that seemed to speak of things she couldn't express. She would often sit by the window, staring out at the horizon as though she were waiting for something—or someone. Julian had always wondered what she was waiting for. She had everything—wealth, beauty, a family—but there was an emptiness in her eyes that Julian couldn't explain.

One evening, when Julian was fifteen, he had overheard a conversation between his parents. He had been coming down the stairs, hoping to ask his father about something, but the voices in the living room stopped him in his tracks.

"I can't do this anymore, Robert," his mother's voice trembled with emotion. "I can't pretend that everything is fine when it's not. We've built an empire, but we've lost each other along the way."

Robert Hart's voice was low, but Julian could hear the edge of irritation in his tone. "What are you saying, Elena?"

"I'm saying that I'm not happy," she replied, her voice barely above a whisper. "I love you, but I can't keep living in this gilded cage. I need more than just wealth. I need a connection, Robert. I need to feel something real."

The words had hit Julian like a slap in the face. He had never heard his mother speak like this before. She had always been so composed, so perfect. But now, in that moment, she sounded fragile—like something was breaking inside her.

His father was silent for a long time before he spoke again. "You know how important this is to me, Elena. The legacy, the empire we've built—it's everything. If we lose that, we lose everything."

"I don't want to lose you, Robert," his mother had said, her voice breaking. "But I feel like I've lost myself."

Julian had retreated to his room after that, his heart pounding in his chest. He had never understood the depth of his mother's unhappiness, nor had he realized how much his father's obsession with success had affected their family. The argument was just another piece of the puzzle, another reminder of the price that had to be paid for the life they had. And it was a price that

Julian had never wanted to pay, not for love, not for happiness, not for anything.

—-

As Julian stood in the park, the weight of those memories settled heavily on his shoulders. His past—his family, his upbringing, his relationship with both of his parents—had shaped him into the man he was today. A man who had everything in terms of wealth, but nothing when it came to real connection. His father's expectations, his mother's quiet sorrow, had left him with an unshakable feeling of emptiness. It was a void that no amount of money could fill.

The wind picked up, rustling the leaves of the trees around him, and for a moment, Julian felt the need to run—to escape the past that had followed him here. But he knew it wouldn't work. The past was always with him, lurking just beneath the surface, ready to resurface at any moment.

And then, as if in response to his thoughts, his phone buzzed in his pocket. Julian fished it out, the sudden interruption breaking his reverie. The screen lit up with a message from Greg, his former assistant, the one person still tethered to the life he had left behind.

"Mr. Hart, your father's asking about you. He's upset you've been gone so long. He wants to know when you'll be coming back to the office."

Julian stared at the screen, his thumb hovering over the keyboard. His father. Even now, even after all these years, the expectations were still there. The pressure to return, to step back into his old life, was never far behind. But Julian felt a deep unease in the pit of his stomach. He had come here to escape that very thing—to escape the life that had shaped him into someone he didn't even recognize.

With a deep breath, he turned off his phone and stuffed it back into his pocket. The past was behind him, but it wasn't finished with him yet. He had to face it, no matter how much it hurt. Because if he didn't, it would continue to haunt him forever.

As the sun began to set, casting long shadows across the park, Julian made a silent vow to himself. He wasn't going back to the life he had known. Not yet. Not until he could prove, once and for all, that there was more to him than the man his family had made him. And he would start with Clara.

Four

A Bond Forms

The rain had stopped, but the air remained thick with moisture. The streets of the small town glistened beneath the streetlights as Julian made his way back to the café. It had become something of a refuge for him, a place where he could temporarily escape the relentless pressure of his past and the harsh reality of the life he had chosen to live. But it was more than that now. It had become a place where Clara existed—where he could see her without the weight of his own deception pressing down on him.

He had been visiting the café daily, always at the same time, hoping to find her. The first time she had spoken to him, Julian hadn't been sure what to expect. She had caught him off guard, her genuine interest in him, a stranger, making him feel like he was seeing the world through fresh eyes. There was no pretense, no hidden agendas. Just a quiet, simple connection.

As Julian entered the café, he felt the familiar warmth envelop him. The low hum of conversations, the clink of coffee cups, and the soft jazz music playing in the background created a sense of comfort that he hadn't realized he was missing. He glanced around the room, his eyes scanning for her. And there she was, sitting at the same table by the window, a book in her hands and a cup of coffee beside her. Her hair was loosely tied back, and she looked as effortlessly beautiful as ever.

For a moment, Julian stood frozen, watching her. He couldn't help it—she had this way of making everything seem easy, effortless. It was as though the world, with all its complications, was far away when she was near. He could feel his heart beat a little faster, but this time, it wasn't out of anxiety. It was because of the pull she had on him, the one he couldn't explain.

He walked toward her, trying to quell the unease bubbling inside him. He had been so careful up until now. He had kept his true identity locked away, and every moment spent with Clara had been one where he carefully measured his words, where he gave only small pieces of himself—never enough to reveal the truth. But the connection between them had been growing stronger, pulling him in, and the mask he had worn for so long was beginning to crack. He wasn't sure how much longer he could keep pretending.

"Hey, Clara," Julian said, his voice steady, though there was a faint tremor in his chest. "Mind if I join you?"

Clara looked up from her book, her lips curling into that warm smile that always made his stomach flip. "Of course, Jack. Pull up a chair." She motioned to the seat across from her.

Julian took the seat, trying to steady himself. The air between them felt charged, and he wasn't sure if it was because of his growing feelings for her or the guilt gnawing at the back of his mind. Clara didn't know the truth. She didn't know that he wasn't just some regular guy passing through—she didn't know that he was Julian Hart, heir to a fortune, a man whose life had been defined by wealth and status. She didn't know that he had been hiding from his past, living a life of disguise.

And yet, despite all of that, Clara still made him feel like he mattered. Like he was more than just his money.

She closed her book and set it aside, her gaze lingering on him. "How was your day?" she asked, her voice soft and inviting.

Julian gave a small, unsteady laugh. "You know, the usual. Worked at the bookstore, ran a few errands. Nothing too exciting."

Clara raised an eyebrow. "You know, I have to admit, I don't think I've ever met anyone who works as many odd jobs as you. What's the deal with that? Most people would be satisfied with one job. Why all the hustle?"

Julian hesitated, trying to figure out how to answer without revealing too much. The truth was, he hadn't been able to sit still since arriving in the town. He had tried to lose himself in the monotony of work, hoping that it would numb the gnawing emptiness inside him. But it hadn't worked. No matter what job he took on, no matter how many hours he spent at the bookstore or the café, the questions kept coming. Why was he doing this? What was he really searching for?

"I don't know," he said finally, his voice quiet. "I guess I've always felt like I needed to keep moving. Always working, always doing something... like I'm running away from something, even though I don't really know what it is."

Clara leaned forward slightly, her eyes studying him with an intensity that made him feel exposed. "I think I understand. Sometimes, it feels like we're all running from something, doesn't it? But maybe the trick is to stop running and just... let ourselves be, for once."

Her words struck a chord deep within him. It was the first time anyone had ever said something so simple, yet so profound. Julian felt a pang in his chest, the weight of his past pressing in on him. He had been running for so long—running from his family, from the expectations, from the life that had been forced upon him. But Clara... Clara made it sound so easy. Just stop running. Just be.

He swallowed hard, the words almost escaping his lips before he could stop them. "I think I'm tired of running."

Clara smiled softly, as though she understood, as though she could see through the walls he had carefully built around himself. "Well, Jack, you've got to give yourself permission to stop. Life isn't just about work or constantly moving. It's about finding something that makes you feel... grounded, you know?"

Julian nodded, though he didn't fully understand what she meant. Grounded. What did that even feel like? He had spent so long in a world of constant motion, always chasing after the next big thing, the next opportunity, the next deal. But here, in this small town, with Clara, he felt something different. Something he hadn't felt in years. Peace. Maybe even hope.

For the next few hours, they talked about everything and nothing. Clara shared stories about her childhood, about her love for painting, and about the dream she had of one day opening her own gallery. She spoke with such passion, her eyes lighting up whenever she talked about her art, and Julian found himself hanging on every word. It was so easy to talk to her, so natural. The world outside seemed to fall away whenever she was near, and he felt... lighter. For the first time since arriving in town, he felt like he could truly be himself.

As the evening wore on, the café began to empty, the chatter dying down as the last few patrons finished their drinks and left. The lights above flickered softly, casting a warm glow over the room. It was then that Julian realized how much time had passed. He had spent hours with Clara, and yet it felt like only moments.

Clara stretched, yawning slightly. "I should probably get going. I have an early morning tomorrow."

Julian nodded, reluctantly standing up. "Yeah, I guess I should head out too."

They walked to the door together, and as Clara stepped out into the cool night air, she turned to him, her expression thoughtful. "Jack, I'm glad you came tonight. I don't know what it is, but… I feel like we've known each other a lot longer than we really have."

Julian's heart skipped a beat. Her words were like a balm to the wound he had been carrying for so long. She didn't know who he really was, but in that moment, it didn't matter. There was something in her words, something in the way she looked at him, that made him feel like he mattered.

"I'm glad too," Julian said quietly, his voice thick with emotion. "I… I'm glad I met you, Clara."

She smiled softly, a smile that seemed to reach her eyes and warm him from the inside out. "Good night, Jack. I'll see you tomorrow."

Julian watched her walk away, his chest tight with a mixture of emotions he didn't know how to process. He had spent so long hiding from the world, hiding from the truth, that he had almost forgotten what it felt like to connect with another person. But Clara had made him feel seen—like he was more than just the sum of his mistakes, more than just the wealth he had abandoned.

As he walked away, his mind was flooded with questions. How long could he keep up the facade? How long before the truth came out? But as he walked down the empty street, a sense of calm washed over him. For the first time in years, he wasn't thinking about the future or the past. He was simply living in the moment, and for the first time, it felt like enough.

Five

The Secret Unveiled

The town was quiet under the veil of twilight, the air cool and fresh with the scent of damp earth after the rain. Julian made his way down the narrow streets, his thoughts heavy and tangled, each step growing more burdened with the weight of the lie he had been living. He had spent the last few weeks with Clara, sharing his time with her in a way that felt more real than anything he had experienced in years. She had become a steady presence in his life, a reminder of the simple joys of human connection. But beneath it all, the truth gnawed at him, a constant ache in his chest, a secret that he could no longer ignore.

The truth. It was a word he had avoided, a concept he had pushed to the back of his mind as he crafted a new identity for himself. But with each passing day, it felt more and more like a ticking clock—an inevitable explosion waiting to happen.

Clara deserved the truth. She deserved to know who he really was, not the carefully constructed mask he had put on to hide from the world.

But the fear… the fear of losing her was almost too much to bear.

Julian had never been good at vulnerability. His entire life had been built on control, on power, on keeping people at arm's length so they couldn't hurt him. But Clara was different. She was the first person in a long time who had seen through the walls he had built. She had no idea who he really was, but she had seen something in him—a man who was trying to escape the prison of his own making.

As he reached the café, his heart began to race. He had arranged to meet Clara there, hoping that a quiet evening would give him the chance to finally tell her the truth. But now, standing in front of the café, he wasn't sure he was ready. He wasn't sure if he could bear to see the hurt in her eyes when she found out who he really was. He had lied to her—kept secrets that she didn't deserve.

His hand hovered over the door, and for a moment, he considered walking away. But then, the sound of Clara's voice reached him from inside. She was laughing, her bright, melodic laughter filling the space around him, and it anchored him in that moment. He couldn't walk away now. Not when he was so close. He had to tell her. He had to face the consequences of his actions.

Taking a deep breath, Julian pushed open the door and stepped inside.

The café was dimly lit, the golden glow from the hanging lights casting a warm, inviting atmosphere. Clara was seated at their usual table by the window, a book in her hands, her eyes focused on the pages. She looked up as she heard the door open, her face breaking into a smile as she saw him standing there.

"Jack!" she said, her voice soft and welcoming. "You made it. I wasn't sure if you were still coming."

Julian's heart clenched at the sound of her voice. How had he let it get this far? How had he allowed himself to become so attached to someone who didn't even know who he truly was?

"I'm sorry I'm late," he said, walking toward her. "Got caught up with work. You know how it is."

Clara closed her book and set it aside, her eyes gleaming with interest. "No worries. I'm just glad you're here. I missed our talks."

The words stung more than he expected. Missed our talks. She didn't know how much those talks had meant to him. She didn't know how much of a lifeline she had become in a world that felt empty without her.

Julian sat down across from her, forcing a smile. He wanted to reach out, to touch her hand, but he couldn't bring himself to do it. The weight of his secret was too heavy, too overwhelming.

"I missed them too," he said quietly.

They sat in silence for a moment, the quiet hum of the café wrapping around them. Julian could feel the tension building, the words he had been avoiding pressing on him like a vice. He had to say it. He had to tell her.

"Clara," he began, his voice shaky. "There's something I need to tell you."

Clara raised an eyebrow, her expression shifting to one of curiosity. "What is it, Jack? You're starting to look all serious on me. What's going on?"

He took a deep breath, his chest tightening. "I'm not who you think I am."

Clara blinked, her smile faltering for a split second. "What do you mean?"

Julian swallowed hard, the words choking him as they fought their way to the surface. "I… I'm not just some guy passing through. I'm not who I told you I was. My name isn't Jack."

Clara's brow furrowed, her confusion growing. "What do you mean? You're not Jack? Then… who are you?"

He looked down at the table, his hands trembling slightly as he gripped the edge. "My real name is Julian Hart. I'm… I'm not just some guy with a normal life. I'm—" He hesitated, the words catching in his throat. "I'm a billionaire. My family… they built an empire. I… I have everything."

The silence between them was deafening. Clara's eyes widened as she processed his words, her expression flickering between disbelief and confusion. Julian could feel his heart pounding in his chest, the weight of his confession hanging in the air like a storm cloud.

"You're a… a billionaire?" Clara repeated, her voice barely above a whisper.

Julian nodded, his stomach twisting in knots. "I've been living a lie, Clara. I've been hiding from my past, from everything I was. I thought… I thought if I could escape, if I could be someone else, I could find something real. I thought maybe you'd see me for who I am, not for my money. But I've been lying to you this whole time."

Clara stared at him, her mouth slightly open, as though she couldn't quite grasp the words he had just spoken. Julian could see the shift in her eyes, the realization dawning on her. The truth was out, and there was no taking it back.

"I didn't want to tell you like this," Julian continued, his voice breaking. "I didn't want to lose what we have. But I can't keep lying to you. I can't keep hiding."

Clara remained silent, her gaze fixed on him, her eyes unreadable. Julian felt as though he were drowning, his words lost in the heavy silence between them. He had hoped—no, prayed—that she would understand, that she would see past his mistakes.

But as the minutes dragged on, the weight of her silence became unbearable.

Finally, Clara spoke, her voice soft but steady. "Why didn't you tell me sooner?"

Julian flinched at the question. "I was afraid," he admitted, his voice barely a whisper. "Afraid you'd hate me. Afraid you'd think I was just another rich guy who didn't care about anything other than his money. But that's not who I am. Not anymore."

Clara stood up suddenly, her chair scraping against the floor. Julian's heart skipped a beat as she took a step back, her face flushed with emotion. "You think I'd hate you?" she asked, her voice rising. "You think that's what this is about? I don't care about your money, Julian. I never did. But you've been lying to me. For weeks. You've been pretending to be someone you're not. And now, I don't even know who you really are."

Julian felt the sting of her words, each one cutting deeper than he had anticipated. He wanted to reach out, to apologize, to beg for her forgiveness, but the space between them felt insurmountable. The truth had shattered everything.

Clara turned toward the door, her face a mixture of hurt and disbelief. "I need some time, Julian. I don't know if I can trust you anymore."

And with that, she walked out of the café, leaving Julian alone with the pieces of a lie that had once felt like his only escape.

Six

The Arrival of the Ex-Girlfriend

The wind had shifted, turning colder as Julian made his way through the quiet streets of the town. His footsteps were muffled by the thick layer of fallen leaves that crunched beneath his boots, and the sky overhead was a deep gray, as though it too were mourning the events of the past few days. Clara hadn't spoken to him since the night of the revelation, and Julian's attempts to reach out had been met with silence. Each message he sent, each call he made, was left unanswered, as though she had vanished into thin air. He couldn't blame her—he had destroyed whatever fragile trust they had built, shattered it with one confession.

The truth had been a wedge between them, and Clara had chosen to walk away. Julian had always known that he was a man capable of running from things—his family, his wealth, his identity—but now he realized, with a gut-wrenching certainty, that the one thing he had tried hardest to run from was the only thing that had ever truly mattered: love.

He glanced up at the café as he walked by. It had become a painful reminder of what he had lost—of the conversations he had shared with Clara, of the way she had smiled at him as though he were something more than a rich man hiding from his own life. He had ruined it. And now, he didn't know if he could ever get it back.

As he passed, a familiar voice cut through the quiet evening air. His heart skipped a beat, the hairs on the back of his neck standing on end as he turned toward the sound.

"Julian?"

He froze.

There, standing in the doorway of the café, was Vanessa. His ex-girlfriend. The last person he had expected—or wanted—to see in this town.

Vanessa's presence hit him like a physical blow. Her tall frame, the perfect poise she had carried since he first met her, and the cold, calculating look in her eyes reminded him of everything he had left behind. Everything he had tried to escape.

"What are you doing here?" Julian's voice was low, almost a growl, but it didn't escape the tightness in his chest. Vanessa had always known how to make him feel trapped, as if she held all the strings that tethered him to the life he was trying to forget.

“I could ask you the same thing,” Vanessa replied, a smile playing at the corner of her lips, but it was cold. “I never thought I’d find you in a place like this.”

“I’m just passing through,” Julian said quickly, hoping his tone would close the conversation. He turned to leave, but Vanessa was already walking toward him, her heels clicking against the pavement in a rhythm that felt like a countdown to something he couldn’t control.

“Passing through?” She arched an eyebrow, her eyes scanning him with a sharpness that sent a chill down his spine. “I don’t believe that for a second.”

Julian swallowed hard. “What do you want, Vanessa?”

“I want to know why you disappeared,” she said, her voice turning hard. “You just left, without a word. No warning. No explanation. It’s been months, Julian.”

“I needed a break,” he said, his words clipped. He didn’t want to go back to that life—the life where Vanessa had been a constant, where her presence had been more of a contract than a relationship. She had never cared about him—at least not in the way he had hoped. She had only cared about what he could give her.

Vanessa stepped closer, narrowing the distance between them. “A break? Is that really what you call it?” Her eyes were intense now, her gaze never leaving his face. "I think you left because you were bored. I think you left because, deep down, you knew we were never going to work."

Julian looked at her, his mind reeling with a mix of anger and disbelief. "We were never going to work because you never cared about me," he said, his voice rising. "You only cared about my name. About my wealth. About what I could give you. You never saw me for who I am."

Vanessa smiled coldly, as if she had won some silent battle. "Maybe you're right, Julian. But you're not the man you think you are. You think that walking away from everything will change who you are inside, but it won't. You're still the same man who hid behind his money. And that's the man I knew."

Julian's hands balled into fists at his sides, his frustration and anger building. "I'm not that man anymore," he said, his voice low but firm. "I'm not him. Not anymore."

Vanessa stepped closer, her lips curling into a smile that didn't reach her eyes. "I can see that. You're hiding here, pretending to be someone you're not, hoping no one will find out. But I know the truth, Julian. I know what you really are."

The sting of her words landed hard, and for a moment, Julian found himself speechless. She was right about one thing. He had been hiding. Hiding from his family, hiding from the life he had known, and—most painfully—hiding from the truth about himself. But this wasn't about her anymore. This wasn't about the woman he had once been with. This was about something far more important. Something that was slipping through his fingers because of his own mistakes.

"I don't need your approval anymore, Vanessa," he said finally, his voice hard. "And I don't need to prove myself to you."

She laughed, the sound as hollow as ever. "Oh, you don't need my approval, Julian? How convenient. But you'll need something, won't you? You'll need someone to help you clean up your mess." Her gaze flickered to the café behind him, and Julian followed her eyes, realizing for the first time how much of their conversation had drawn the attention of a few passersby.

"I don't want anything from you," Julian said, shaking his head, his voice tight. "I'm done with the games, Vanessa. I'm done pretending."

Vanessa's expression shifted for just a second, a flicker of something—regret, perhaps—crossing her face, before she quickly masked it. "You're not done pretending," she said softly. "You're just learning how to lie better. You think you've escaped, but you haven't. You're still trapped, Julian. You always will be."

Before he could respond, she turned sharply and walked away, her heels clicking against the pavement, each step farther away from him. Julian stood frozen, watching her go, feeling the remnants of her presence linger in the air.

—-

The next few days were a blur. Julian tried to push Vanessa from his mind, but the truth was, her arrival had done more than just shake him. It had shattered the fragile sense of control he had managed to hold on to since he'd come to the town. The lies, the masks he had worn for so long, were no longer enough. The encounter with Vanessa made him realize something he had been trying to deny: he was still running. He was still hiding from his past, and it would always follow him.

He had gone to the café that day, hoping that Clara might be there, hoping for some sign that he could fix what he had broken. But Clara was still gone. No calls, no messages. The silence from her side was deafening, and every attempt to reach out felt like another nail in the coffin of whatever had once been between them.

That night, as Julian walked back to the small apartment he had rented, he caught sight of a figure in the distance—a shadow just beyond the streetlamp. He recognized the silhouette instantly. It was Clara.

His heart skipped a beat as he walked toward her, his footsteps faster now, a mix of hope and dread tightening in his chest. He had to talk to her. He had to make her understand.

"Clara!" he called, his voice shaking slightly. She stopped, but didn't turn around. He could see her stiffen, her body language closing off, as if she was bracing herself for what was coming. He stepped closer, his eyes searching her face, but her expression was unreadable.

"Clara, please..." His voice faltered, and he took another step forward, desperate for a chance to explain, to fix things.

"I don't want to hear it, Julian," she said softly, her voice barely audible over the quiet hum of the street. She still hadn't turned to face him, and that hurt more than anything.

He swallowed hard, the weight of her rejection almost too much to bear. "Please, just give me a chance to explain. I've made mistakes, but I'm not the man I was before. I'm not him."

Clara finally turned to face him, her expression soft, but there was sadness in her eyes that made Julian's stomach drop. "You lied to me, Julian," she said, her voice barely above a whisper. "And I don't know if I can trust you again. Not after everything."

The words hung in the air like a cold wind, and Julian's heart shattered all over again. But before he could respond, Clara turned and walked away, disappearing into the shadows of the night, leaving him standing there, his heart heavy with the weight of his own mistakes.

And then, like the storm it was, Vanessa's words returned to him: You think you've escaped, but you haven't. You're still trapped, Julian. You always will be.

Seven

The Web of Lies

The clock on the wall ticked in the quiet apartment, its hands moving forward in a slow, relentless march, marking each passing second with an almost mocking precision. Julian sat in the dimly lit living room, his fingers gripping the glass of whiskey in front of him, but his eyes were fixed on the empty space across the room, where Clara had once sat. It had been days since their last confrontation, and the silence between them had become a suffocating presence. He had told her the truth, but it felt like he was drowning in the lies that had built up around him.

He had tried calling her. He had left messages, sent texts, even tried reaching her through mutual acquaintances. But there had been nothing—no reply, no sign of her. The silence was a painful reminder of the distance that now separated them, the chasm that he had created with one simple confession. He had known it would be hard, that she would be hurt, but he hadn't anticipated the weight of it—the feeling that he had lost her forever.

The whiskey burned in his throat as he took another drink, trying to numb the thoughts swirling in his head. The web of lies he had woven was so tangled, so complicated, that it felt impossible to untangle. And the worst part was, he didn't even know where to begin. He had been living a life of deception for so long that the truth felt like a foreign concept, something he was barely able to grasp anymore.

As he sat there, lost in his own thoughts, his phone buzzed on the coffee table. He glanced at it, the name on the screen making his stomach churn. Greg. His former assistant. The one person who had always been a constant presence in his life, someone who knew the real Julian Hart. The person who had helped him navigate the world of business, the one who had always been at his side when he needed guidance.

Julian's finger hovered over the phone for a moment, and then, with a sense of inevitability, he answered.

"Julian," Greg's voice came through, as crisp and efficient as always. "We need to talk."

The words were simple, but they sent a shiver down Julian's spine. There was something in Greg's tone that suggested urgency, something that made Julian's heart race in his chest.

"What is it, Greg?" Julian asked, trying to keep his voice

steady, but there was a tremor there, something that he couldn't quite hide. He had been waiting for this moment, had known it was coming, but he wasn't sure he was ready to face the consequences.

"There's a problem," Greg said, his voice lowering. "A big one. Your father's been asking about you. He's looking into the fact that you've been gone for so long, and he's… well, he's not happy."

Julian's heart skipped a beat. His father. The man who had built the empire that Julian was supposed to inherit. The man who had never cared for anything other than success and power. Julian had hoped that by leaving, he could escape the suffocating expectations that his father had placed on him. But now, it seemed, his father's grip was tightening again.

"What does he want?" Julian asked, his voice barely above a whisper.

Greg sighed. "He wants you back, Julian. He wants you to come home, to take your place in the company. He's making all sorts of threats if you don't come back. And he's even mentioned… bringing in people to find you."

A cold wave of fear washed over Julian. His father had always been a man of action, a man who didn't hesitate to use whatever means necessary to get what he wanted. Julian had known this. He had grown up in the shadow of it. But now, as the reality of it settled in, he realized just how deep the web of lies had gotten. He had been hiding from his father, hiding from his past, but now it seemed like there was no escaping it.

"I'll handle it," Julian said, his voice low, more to himself than to Greg. He didn't know how he would handle it. He didn't know how he could possibly go back to that life, that world of wealth and power that had never felt like his own.

"There's more," Greg said, his voice tightening. "I've been getting some strange calls. People asking about your business ventures, your assets. Someone's digging into your finances, Julian. They're looking for something."

Julian stood up abruptly, the glass of whiskey slipping from his hand and shattering on the floor. He didn't hear it. He didn't care. His mind was racing, his pulse hammering in his ears. Someone's looking for something. The words echoed in his mind, sending a jolt of panic through his body. He had spent years building up a life that was based on lies, based on deception. And now it was all starting to unravel.

"Who is it?" Julian demanded, his voice tight. "Who's looking for me?"

Greg was silent for a moment, and Julian could hear the hesitation in his voice when he spoke again.

"I don't know," Greg said slowly. "But it's not just your father. There's someone else—someone with a lot of power, someone who's trying to find out everything about you. And they won't stop until they get what they want."

Julian's breath caught in his throat. His mind flashed back to his life before he had left—to the deals he had made, the people he had crossed. The enemies he had made in the pursuit of wealth, power, and success. He had always thought he could outrun them, always thought he could hide. But now, it seemed like the past was catching up with him faster than he could outrun it.

"What do you want me to do?" Julian asked, his voice barely a whisper, his thoughts spinning.

Greg hesitated before responding. "I think you need to come back, Julian. I think it's the only way to stop whatever's coming. You can't keep running from this. You can't keep hiding."

Julian didn't answer immediately. He couldn't. He had spent years running from the life he had been born into, from the man he was supposed to become. But now, as the walls closed in around him, he realized that there was nowhere left to hide. The web of lies he had woven was too tangled, and it was pulling him back into the life he had tried so hard to escape.

"I'll think about it," Julian said finally, his voice hollow. "I'll let you know."

He ended the call without another word and stood there in the center of the room, the pieces of his shattered glass still scattered on the floor around him. His heart was racing, his thoughts a whirlwind of fear, guilt, and frustration. He had tried to escape. He had tried to leave behind everything that had made him who he was. But now, it seemed like there was no escaping the truth.

As he sank into the armchair, his mind kept returning to Clara. The hurt in her eyes, the disbelief that had flashed across her face when she had learned the truth about him—it haunted him. She had been the one person who had made him believe that maybe, just maybe, he could escape his past, that he could build something real with her. But now, that too was slipping away.

The web of lies had pulled him back in. And no matter how hard he tried to break free, it seemed like the past would always find a way to pull him under.

He closed his eyes, running a hand through his hair in frustration. He had to make a decision. He couldn't keep running. He had to face whatever was coming, even if it meant going back to the life he had tried to forget. But as the weight of his choices settled in, he realized that there was no easy way out. No matter what he did, no matter how much he tried to outrun it, the web of lies would always find a way to entangle him. And when it did, there would be no escaping the consequences.

Eight

A Test of Trust

The days had blurred into each other, like the raindrops falling endlessly against the window panes, relentless and unyielding. Julian hadn't left his apartment in three days. He had tried, several times, to reach Clara, but his messages had gone unanswered. Every call went to voicemail. The silence was deafening, a sharp reminder of the rift that had opened between them, one he had created with a single revelation. The truth.

He had told Clara everything—the truth about who he was, about the life he had lived, and the one he had tried to escape. It had been a necessary step, one he knew would eventually come to this. But now that the truth was out, he was left with a question he couldn't escape: Had it been worth it?

Julian had never understood the fragility of trust, never realized how quickly it could fracture, until it happened to him. The foundation of everything he had built with Clara had crumbled in an instant. He could still remember the hurt in her eyes, the disbelief, and the anger that had rippled through her as the weight of his confession sank in. She had trusted him, and he had betrayed that trust.

It had been a test of trust, one that had backfired in the most painful way possible. And now, Clara was gone. And so was the future he had dared to imagine with her.

He stood by the window, his hands pressed against the cool glass as he stared out at the gray, rain-soaked streets. The town was eerily quiet, the usual bustle of people going about their lives muted under the heavy downpour. It was as though the world outside was holding its breath, waiting for something to happen. Waiting for him to make a decision.

He had tried to run from the truth for so long, to hide behind a mask of lies and pretenses. But now, the mask was gone. And with it, the illusion that he could escape from the life he had been born into.

The phone on the table buzzed, snapping Julian out of his reverie. He glanced at it, his heart skipping a beat when he saw the name on the screen.

Clara.

He didn't know how long he had been staring at the screen, but the realization hit him like a punch to the gut. It had been days since he'd last heard from her. And now, she was calling him? He hesitated, his thumb hovering over the screen, unsure of what to do. What could he possibly say to her? He had already told her everything. He had bared his soul, hoping for understanding, hoping for a second chance. But that hope had been dashed, and now he was left with nothing but the consequences of his actions.

But then the phone rang again, and Julian made a decision. He answered it.

"Clara?" His voice was rough, tentative, as though he were afraid the phone would cut off at any moment.

There was a pause on the other end of the line. And then, her voice—soft, cautious—spoke.

"Julian… we need to talk."

Julian's chest tightened. He had hoped for this moment, but now that it was here, he didn't know what to say. He wasn't prepared for the possibility of forgiveness. He wasn't prepared for what would come next. All he knew was that he couldn't lose her. Not now, not when everything felt so fragile.

"I know I've hurt you," he said, his voice steady but thick with emotion. "I never meant to. I never wanted to hurt you."

"I know you didn't," Clara replied quietly. "But the truth… it's a lot to process, Julian. I don't know if I can just move past it."

"I know," Julian said, his throat tightening. "I didn't think it would be easy. But I can't keep living with the lie. I couldn't keep hiding it from you."

Clara was silent for a moment, and Julian's heart raced as he waited for her to respond. Every second felt like an eternity, each one building the tension that hung between them. He could feel the weight of her decision hanging in the air, could almost hear the wheels turning in her mind as she tried to make sense of everything.

Finally, she spoke again. "I need to know that you're not just the man I saw that night. I need to know that you're the person you say you are. Not the one who hides behind his wealth. Not the one who lies to everyone, including himself. I need to trust you again, Julian."

Her words struck him like a blade, sharp and precise. The test of trust wasn't just about her forgiving him—it was about him proving that he had changed, that he wasn't the man he had been before. It was about him showing her that the man who had lied, the man who had hidden behind his riches, was no longer who he was.

And that, Julian realized, was the hardest part.

"I can prove it," he said, the words escaping before he could think them through. "I can show you who I really am, Clara. I can show you the man I want to be. But I need you to trust me. To give me a chance."

There was a long pause, and Julian held his breath, waiting for her response. The silence between them felt suffocating, as though the very air they were breathing was thick with unspoken words, unacknowledged fears. Finally, Clara spoke again.

"Okay," she said, her voice barely a whisper. "I'll give you a chance. But you need to prove it to me, Julian. You need to show me that you're not just a mask. That you're someone I can believe in."

Julian closed his eyes, relief flooding through him in waves. It wasn't forgiveness—not yet—but it was a chance. A chance to prove that he was worthy of her trust. A chance to show her that the man who had walked into her life wasn't a lie.

"I won't let you down," he said, his voice filled with conviction. "I'll show you that I'm not who I was."

—-

The next few days were a blur of frantic energy and uncertainty. Julian found himself thrust into a whirlwind of activity, scrambling to fix the mess he had made, to piece together the trust that had been shattered. But with each passing hour, he began to realize that regaining Clara's trust wasn't going to be easy. She wasn't going to just forgive him because he wanted it. She wasn't going to erase the hurt he had caused with a simple apology.

No, he had to show her. He had to prove to her, with actions, that he was no longer the man he had been. The man who hid behind his wealth and his lies. The man who had believed that love could be bought.

Julian found himself walking through the streets of the town, his mind whirling with possibilities. He had to make things right, somehow. He had to show Clara that he was worthy of the chance she had given him.

His first step was to visit the local bookstore. It was the first place Clara had taken him, the place where they had first connected. He had always known that she loved books—had always known that they were an escape for her, a way for her to find peace in a world that often didn't make sense. He walked inside, the bell above the door jingling as he entered, and he asked the clerk about a specific book.

It was a rare edition of one of Clara's favorite authors, one that she had mentioned casually during one of their many conversations. It was a book she had always wanted but could never find. He knew she would never expect him to remember it. But he had.

He bought the book, carefully wrapped it in plain brown paper, and left the store, his heart pounding with anticipation. This was his first step. A small gesture, perhaps, but it was a step toward rebuilding the trust that had been so carelessly shattered.

—-

That evening, Julian waited outside the café, the book tucked carefully under his arm. He had no idea if Clara would show up. He didn't know if she would even be willing to talk to him. But he had to try. He had to make it clear that he wasn't just some rich man playing at a different life. He was someone who cared. Someone who wanted to be better—not just for her, but for himself.

The rain had stopped, and the sky was clear, the stars shining down on the town like tiny pinpricks of light. Julian paced back and forth, waiting, the minutes stretching endlessly. Finally, after what seemed like an eternity, Clara walked into view, her figure framed by the soft glow of the café's lights.

She saw him immediately, and for a moment, they just stood there, locked in place. She hadn't said a word since their conversation, but Julian could see the guarded look in her eyes, the hesitation in the way she moved toward him.

He stepped forward, holding out the wrapped book. "Clara," he said softly. "I know this won't fix everything, but I wanted you to have this. It's a small gesture, but it's a start."

Clara hesitated, her gaze flickering from the book to his face. Her lips parted, but she didn't speak immediately. Finally, she took the book from his hands, her fingers brushing against his as she did.

She looked up at him, her expression unreadable. "It's a start," she repeated quietly. And for the first time in days, Julian saw a flicker of hope in her eyes.

It wasn't forgiveness, not yet. But it was a beginning. And that, Julian realized, was all he needed.

Nine

The Heart's Dilemma

The wind howled through the streets, bending the trees and causing the leaves to swirl like fragments of the past—catching moments in its unforgiving current. The sky, once clear, now loomed dark and heavy, an ominous backdrop for the internal storm brewing inside Julian's chest. He stood by the window in his apartment, staring out at the chaotic scene, but his thoughts were far away, fixed on one singular question: What did she really want from him?

Clara had taken the book. That was the only thing he knew for sure. She had taken it, but she hadn't said a word since. Her expression when she accepted it had been unreadable—guarded. As if she were considering something far beyond the simple gesture, weighing something deeper. The flicker of hope in her eyes had been brief, but it had been there. Still, hope alone wasn't enough to bridge the gap that had opened between them.

The rift caused by his lies, by his very existence as a wealthy man, still loomed large, like a dark cloud waiting to release its storm.

For days now, Julian had been lost in this labyrinth of doubt and regret, questioning everything. He had started this journey trying to find redemption, trying to break free from the chains that his money and status had wrapped around him. But now, as he looked at the faint reflection of himself in the glass, he wondered if that had all been in vain. He had given Clara a glimpse of who he truly was, the vulnerable man beneath the mask. But was that enough? Was it ever going to be enough?

The sound of his phone buzzing broke through his thoughts, and Julian glanced down at the screen. A text from Greg.

"Julian, your father wants a meeting. It's urgent."

Julian's stomach tightened. His father. The man who had always been the architect of his life, the one who had built the empire that Julian had never truly wanted to inherit. The man who was now demanding his presence, pulling him back into a life that Julian had so desperately tried to escape.

He could feel the familiar tension in his chest, the weight of his family's expectations pressing on him like a vise. He had been trying to carve a new path for himself, away from his father's influence, away from the suffocating expectations that had ruled his every move. But now, it seemed like that life was crashing back into his reality. The question was: would he choose it? Would he choose his father's world or the fragile, uncertain future with Clara?

Julian knew that he couldn't have both. The two worlds were too far apart, too contradictory. He could already feel the tug in his heart, the way his loyalty to his father fought against the burgeoning desire to prove himself to Clara. She had given him a chance to show her who he really was, but could he truly leave behind everything his father had built?

—-

Clara was still sitting at the café when Julian walked in. Her presence, like always, felt like a quiet force that filled the space. She was hunched over a cup of coffee, her fingers tracing the edge of the cup, her focus intense. It was late, the café empty except for a few scattered customers, the warm light casting a soft glow over her features. For a moment, Julian hesitated in the doorway, watching her as if she were an illusion he could never quite touch.

She hadn't noticed him. And that made him wonder whether that was a blessing or a curse.

It had been over a week since their last conversation. A week since the book. And now here he was, standing in front of her again, no clearer about his own path, but desperate for some kind of answer, even if it wasn't the one he wanted.

He walked toward her, the steps slow, almost reluctant. He could feel his heart pounding in his chest, each step a reminder of the weight of everything he had failed to say, failed to prove.

Clara looked up just as he reached the table, her eyes locking onto his, unreadable. She didn't smile, but there was a quiet recognition there. She hadn't pushed him away. She hadn't turned her back entirely.

"Hey," Julian said, his voice hoarse, unsure of how to begin. His throat tightened as he took the seat opposite her, the distance between them feeling miles apart.

"Hey," Clara replied, her voice soft, but distant, as if she had already made up her mind about something she wasn't ready to share. She placed her cup down, fingers still curled around it as if it were her only anchor in a world that had suddenly become too much.

"I've been thinking," Julian started, then hesitated. He hadn't meant to start like that, but it felt like the only way. "I know I don't deserve it, but I want to prove to you that I'm not the man you think I am."

Clara's brow furrowed, and Julian watched the flicker of emotion cross her face. Something between sadness and curiosity.

"What does that mean, Julian?" she asked, her voice low, searching. "What do you think I think you are?"

He swallowed hard. "I think you see me as the man I've been hiding from. The rich, entitled man who's used money to control everything. The man who thinks he can buy people's love. And that's not who I am anymore. It's never who I wanted to be."

She didn't respond immediately, her fingers still gripping the edge of the cup. Her gaze drifted to the window, and for a moment, Julian thought she might turn away again. But then, she spoke, her voice softer now, but no less firm.

"Julian, I'm not angry at you for being rich," she said slowly, her eyes meeting his once more. "I'm angry at you for not trusting me. For thinking that I wouldn't be able to see past it, that I wouldn't be able to see you."

He flinched. The words stung, but they were true. And that was the hardest part. Clara wasn't angry because of his wealth—she was angry because he had never let her see him for who he truly was. The real man behind the mask.

"I thought... I thought I was protecting you," Julian admitted quietly, his voice barely above a whisper. "I thought if I told you, if you knew the truth about me—who I really am—then you would leave. You would see me as nothing more than my money. As someone who doesn't deserve your love. And I couldn't let that happen."

Clara's expression softened, but there was no warmth in it. Only a kind of painful understanding. "I don't want your money, Julian," she said, the words cutting through the tension like a blade. "I never have. But I needed you to trust me. To show me who you really are, not just the version of you that's been pretending. And I don't know how to move forward if you can't trust me with that."

Her words hit him harder than anything else. In that moment, Julian realized that the real test was never about whether Clara could accept him. It was about whether he could accept himself—the man behind the wealth, the man who had spent his life hiding. It was about trusting her as much as she needed to trust him.

"I want to trust you, Clara," he said, his voice thick with emotion. "I do. But it's hard for me. It's so hard to let go of the only thing I've ever known. The only thing that's ever felt like it mattered."

Clara looked at him then, her eyes soft but resolute. "You have to let go, Julian. You have to let go of your past if you want a future with me. Because I can't live in the shadows of your lies. I can't keep loving someone who's afraid of being real with me."

Julian's heart pounded in his chest. Her words were a challenge, a warning, and a plea all at once. He could feel the weight of it, the pressure building in his chest, as if every breath he took was more difficult than the last. The heart's dilemma wasn't just about choosing between Clara and his father's world. It was about choosing between the man he had become and the man he was still trying to hide from.

He had to make a decision.

And he had to make it now.

"I'm sorry," Julian said, his voice cracking slightly. "I don't know how to be the man you need me to be. But I want to learn. I want to be the man who deserves you. Just... give me time.

Please."

Clara's expression softened, the sadness in her eyes replaced with something else—a glimmer of hope, perhaps, or resignation. "Time is what we don't have, Julian," she said quietly. "But I'll give you a little more. Not for you, but for us."

And in that moment, Julian knew. The test of trust wasn't just about proving himself to Clara—it was about proving to himself that he was worthy of the love that she was offering, the love that had once seemed like an impossible dream. The storm that had raged within him had subsided, but the question remained: would he be brave enough to face it all, to let go of his past, and to build a future with Clara, free from the lies?

The answer was still uncertain, but for the first time in a long time, Julian felt like he was ready to try.

Ten

A Life-Altering Choice

The clock ticked loudly in the silence of the apartment. Julian sat in the center of the room, his hands clenched into fists on his lap, his mind racing, caught between two worlds—one he had fought so desperately to escape, and the other, a fragile chance at a life he never thought possible. The weight of his decision pressed on him, suffocating him with every passing second. Outside, the city buzzed with life, oblivious to the storm raging within him.

He had never felt this torn before. The world he had known—the empire his father had built, the legacy that had been placed in his hands—now felt like a cage, a gilded prison he had tried to leave behind. But that world still had a hold on him, a magnetic pull that he couldn't completely resist. And then, there was Clara—the one person who had made him believe that he could be more than just his wealth, more than the expectations his family had imposed on him.

The choice he had to make wasn't an easy one. It was a choice between duty and desire, between the man he had been and the man he hoped to become. It was a choice that would alter the course of his life forever, and he had no idea which path was the right one.

Julian had spent the past few days in a daze, torn between calls from his father demanding his return to the family business and the quiet whispers of his heart that told him to walk away. His father had never been one to show emotion, but the urgency in his voice had been undeniable. He wanted Julian back at the helm, to take his rightful place in the empire that had been passed down to him.

But what would it mean for Julian to return? To once again be the son of Robert Hart, the billionaire mogul who had built an empire from the ground up? The man who had shaped Julian's life in ways that no amount of money could undo? Could Julian really step back into that world and give up the one thing that had begun to matter more than all of it?

Clara.

She had given him a chance to prove himself. She had given him hope. But she had also made it clear that she couldn't wait forever. She couldn't be with a man who was unwilling to let go of the past, unwilling to break free of the life that had kept him trapped for so long. Clara had been clear in her feelings, her voice soft but firm when she told him she needed him to make a choice: his old life, or her.

The phone rang again, pulling Julian from his thoughts. It was Greg. The familiar name on the screen made his chest tighten, the weight of the decision pressing down on him even harder. He had already ignored several of Greg's calls, unable to face the reality of what was coming. But now, there was no avoiding it.

With a deep breath, Julian answered.

"Julian," Greg's voice was clipped, urgent. "We need to talk. Your father's given you an ultimatum. He's not playing games anymore."

Julian's heart sank, and he leaned back against the couch, his fingers gripping the edge of his phone tightly. "What do you mean?"

"He's sending people," Greg continued, his voice tinged with concern. "He wants you to come back, and if you don't—he's making threats. Your entire inheritance is on the line. He's telling people that he'll cut you out of the will, strip you of everything. You're the heir, Julian, and you're the only one who can lead the company forward."

The words hung in the air, suffocating Julian. His mind raced, his pulse quickening. This was it—the moment he had been dreading. His father was not a man to make idle threats. He had built his empire with blood, sweat, and a relentless pursuit of power, and if Julian didn't return, if he didn't take control of the business, Robert Hart would make sure that the path Julian had chosen would be obliterated.

"And if I don't go back?" Julian's voice was hoarse, the weight of the choice crushing him. "What happens then?"

"Then everything you've ever known is gone," Greg replied bluntly. "The business, the money, the influence—it all goes to someone else. You'll be cut off. No safety net. No nothing."

The silence that followed felt deafening. Julian's head spun. He had known his father was a man of extreme measures, but hearing the cold, hard reality of it made him feel like he was drowning. Could he really give all of that up? Could he walk away from the legacy, the empire, the life he had been born into?

And yet, the thought of going back to that life, to become the man his father wanted him to be, felt like a death sentence. It felt like a betrayal of everything he had learned about himself in the time he had spent away. He had finally begun to see the possibility of something different—something real—and now his father was threatening to pull him back into the very cage that had nearly crushed him.

"Greg," Julian's voice was steady now, but inside, he was a storm. "I need time. I can't make this decision right now."

"Julian, you don't have time," Greg's voice sharpened with impatience. "Your father is on a warpath. You need to make your choice. Soon."

The call ended abruptly, and Julian sat there, the weight of the world pressing down on him. He knew what his father wanted. He wanted control. He wanted Julian to take the reins and keep the empire intact, to keep the business running smoothly so that it could pass on to the next generation.

But Julian couldn't ignore the truth any longer. The empire his father had built was never meant for him. He had spent his entire life following a path laid out by someone else—by a man who had never once asked him what he wanted. And now, with Clara in his life, Julian had finally seen a glimpse of something different, something real. But that something real came with its own sacrifices. Clara had made it clear that she couldn't be with a man who was split between two worlds—one foot in the past, one foot in the future. If Julian wanted her, if he wanted a life with her, he had to make a choice.

The decision wasn't as simple as choosing between money and love. It was about choosing the life he wanted for himself. It was about breaking free from the chains that had bound him to his past. It was about redefining who he was, not based on his father's expectations, but on his own desires.

Julian stood up, his heart pounding in his chest. He walked to the window, staring out at the rain-soaked city below. The lights flickered in the distance, the reflection of his own indecision rippling across the glass. He felt like he was standing on the edge of something—something dangerous, something unknown—and yet, he couldn't bring himself to look away.

He had to choose.

The door to the apartment creaked open, and Julian turned to see Clara standing there, her silhouette framed by the dim light of the hallway. Her eyes met his, and for a moment, everything else faded away.

"You've been thinking about it, haven't you?" she said softly, her voice steady but filled with concern.

Julian didn't answer immediately. Instead, he stepped toward her, his heart hammering in his chest. There was so much he wanted to say, so much he needed to explain. But the words were stuck in his throat, trapped by the weight of the decision before him.

Clara stepped forward, closing the distance between them. She reached out, her hand resting on his arm, and he felt the warmth of her touch, the reminder of the life he wanted, the life he could have if he made the right choice.

"You don't have to decide right now," she said, her voice gentle but firm. "But when you do, it has to be for you. Not for your father. Not for me. For you."

Julian nodded, the truth of her words sinking in. He had spent so long living for other people, for his father, for the expectations that had been placed on him. But now, the choice was his. The future was his.

He turned to the window again, his heart heavy with the weight of the decision. But this time, he felt something different—a spark of clarity, a sense of purpose that had been missing for so long. He knew what he had to do.

"I'll make my choice, Clara," Julian said, his voice steady. "But it won't be because of what anyone else wants. It'll be because of what I want. And I want to be the man who can build a future, not just a legacy."

Clara's eyes softened, and she stepped closer, her hand still resting on his arm. "Then let's build it together, Julian."

And in that moment, Julian knew. The path ahead would be difficult. It would test him in ways he couldn't yet imagine. But it was his choice, and for the first time in his life, he was finally ready to make it.

Eleven

Unforeseen Consequences

The next few days passed in a haze. Julian had made his choice, or at least, he thought he had. The promise he made to Clara had felt like a heavy weight lifting off his shoulders, but the consequences of that promise were beginning to settle in, a slow, creeping dread he couldn't shake.

He had told his father he wouldn't return. He had made it clear that he was done with the family business, with the empire his father had built for him. He had even gone so far as to tell Greg, his loyal assistant, that he was choosing a different path—a life without the burden of wealth and power. Julian had thought that walking away from it all would bring him peace, would allow him to start over with Clara, to build something real. But nothing was ever that simple, was it?

Julian walked through the darkened apartment, each step heavy with the weight of his decision. The silence that had filled the space between him and Clara seemed to have followed him back home, hanging in the air like a thick fog. It had been days since they had talked, and each moment felt like a small eternity. His heart ached with the thought of her, but the fear of what was to come overshadowed his longing.

The doorbell rang suddenly, a sharp sound that pierced the quiet. Julian froze in his tracks, his pulse quickening. He wasn't expecting anyone—certainly not at this hour.

He walked slowly to the door, his thoughts racing. The last thing he needed was more trouble. The consequences of his decision had barely begun to show their teeth, but he could feel them closing in on him, threatening to drag him back into a world he had fought so hard to escape.

When Julian opened the door, it wasn't Clara standing there, but Greg. His assistant's face was tense, his expression grim. Something was wrong, and Julian knew it before Greg even spoke.

"Julian," Greg said, his voice tight, "you need to come with me. Now."

Julian didn't ask questions. He didn't need to. The urgency in Greg's voice told him everything he needed to know. He grabbed his jacket and followed Greg without another word.

They didn't speak during the drive. Greg kept his eyes on the road, his knuckles white against the steering wheel. Julian sat in the passenger seat, his mind racing with possibilities. What had happened? What consequences were waiting for him?

When they arrived, Julian immediately felt the difference. They were no longer in the small town he had tried to make a new life in. They had driven to the outskirts of the city, to a more remote location. A warehouse stood before them, its lights dim and ominous. The place felt abandoned, out of place in a world that had always been controlled, orderly. But now, everything felt like it was about to unravel.

Greg pulled the car into a parking spot near the back entrance. "Stay close," he said. His tone was colder now, almost fearful.

Julian had no time to process what was happening before Greg ushered him inside. The warehouse was vast, the air thick with the smell of metal and concrete. Julian's footsteps echoed against the empty walls as they moved deeper into the building.

There was a group of men gathered in the center of the room, their figures shrouded in shadow. Julian recognized one of them immediately—Richard Caldwell, a business associate of his father. Richard had always been the more ruthless of the two, the one who didn't hesitate to get his hands dirty when it came to securing deals or eliminating threats.

Greg led Julian toward them, his steps measured, careful. Richard looked up as they approached, his eyes narrowing when they settled on Julian.

"So, you've finally come to see us," Richard said, his voice smooth but laced with a threat that hung in the air like poison.

Julian's stomach churned as he took in the scene before him. It wasn't just business. This wasn't some simple meeting to discuss the future of the company. There was something darker at play, something that made Julian's skin crawl.

"What's this about?" Julian asked, trying to keep his voice steady despite the unease pooling in his gut.

Richard stepped forward, his hands clasped behind his back. "Your father gave us an ultimatum, Julian," he said slowly, his eyes gleaming in the dim light. "He's been generous. He's allowed you to walk away from the company. But there are consequences. There are always consequences when someone tries to defy Robert Hart."

Julian's heart raced. He knew where this was going, but hearing it out loud made the fear settle deeper. "What do you mean?" he asked, his voice barely a whisper.

Richard smiled—a cold, predatory grin. "You've made a choice, Julian. And now we're here to make sure you understand the full weight of that choice. You can't just walk away from your family's business. Not without paying the price."

Julian's mind spun. His father's ultimatum hadn't been a simple threat—it was a declaration of war. Robert Hart's empire was not just a business. It was everything to him. And if Julian refused to return, there would be a reckoning.

Richard's eyes flickered to one of the other men standing in the shadows. The man stepped forward, his expression unreadable, his hands tucked into the pockets of his jacket. "You don't understand, Julian," the man said, his voice low. "Your father has ways of dealing with problems. You've made yourself a problem. And now, you need to fix it."

Julian could feel the weight of the words sinking in. There was no escape. No easy way out. He had thought he could simply walk away from it all, make a fresh start with Clara. But now, with the cold reality of his father's power closing in on him, he realized that there were consequences to his actions—consequences he had never fully understood until now.

"Please," Julian said, his voice tight. "I don't want this. I've made my choice. I'm not going back."

Richard's eyes flashed with something dark—something predatory. "You don't get to make choices anymore, Julian. Not when you've crossed your father. Not when you've thrown away everything he's given you."

The man beside Richard stepped forward again, this time holding a briefcase. He opened it slowly, and Julian could see that it wasn't filled with papers, but something much more dangerous. A gun.

Julian's breath caught in his throat. He couldn't believe what he was seeing. This wasn't just a meeting about business. This was about power—about control. His father wasn't just threatening to take everything away. He was prepared to make Julian disappear.

"We can make this go away," Richard said, his voice low and menacing. "All of it. You just have to come back. You have to do what your father wants."

The room seemed to close in around Julian. He could hear the blood rushing in his ears, his mind racing to make sense of what was happening. This wasn't a decision about business. This wasn't even about Clara anymore. This was about survival.

The man with the gun stepped closer, and Julian could feel the cold, suffocating presence of danger closing in on him. He had made a choice, but the consequences were far more than he had anticipated. His decision to walk away from his father's empire wasn't just a matter of pride—it was a matter of life and death.

"Please," Julian said, his voice barely above a whisper. "I don't want to go back. I won't. I'm done."

Richard's smile widened, a cruel twist on his lips. "Then you'll learn what happens to those who defy Robert Hart."

Before Julian could react, Greg stepped forward, his expression unreadable. "Enough," he said sharply. "This isn't the way we do things."

Julian looked at Greg, confused. He had no idea what was happening, what game Greg was playing. But as the tension in the room grew, Julian realized that his assistant was not on his side. He had been caught in a trap—a web of lies that he couldn't escape.

Greg's next words hit Julian like a slap. "Julian, I'm sorry, but this is bigger than both of us."

Julian's heart sank as the weight of the situation crashed down on him. His father had pulled the strings, but now, it was too late. There was no way out. No way to undo the mess he had created. The consequences of his choice had become something far darker than he had ever imagined.

As the gun was raised, Julian felt the cold pressure of inevitability pressing down on him. There was no escape. No way to outrun the past.

And in that moment, Julian understood the true meaning of the word consequences.

Twelve

The Final Test

The cold metal of the gun pressed against his temple, sending a shockwave of adrenaline through Julian's body. His heart hammered in his chest, each beat growing louder, faster, as though it might break free from his ribs at any moment. He had always been able to control his world, control his fate, with money, with power, with influence. But now, standing in a dark, empty warehouse surrounded by shadows, he realized how little control he truly had. How easily his entire life could be snuffed out in an instant.

Richard's voice, low and calculated, cut through the suffocating silence. "You think you can just walk away, Julian? You think you can turn your back on everything your father built? This is bigger than you. This is bigger than your little fantasy of living some simple life."

Julian didn't respond immediately, his mind racing, trying to piece together the fractured thoughts in his head. His gaze flickered from Richard's cold, unfeeling eyes to the barrel of the gun pressed against his skin. He could feel the dampness of the metal, could hear the faint click of the safety being released. There was no escaping this. He had made his choice, and now, he was going to pay the price.

But even as fear gripped him, a small voice in the back of his mind told him one thing: Don't show them your fear. Don't let them see you break.

"You don't scare me, Richard," Julian said, his voice steadier than he felt. He swallowed hard, forcing the words out. "If you're going to kill me, then do it. Get it over with."

Richard's eyes narrowed, the faintest trace of amusement crossing his face. "You think you have the luxury of talking your way out of this? Your father's empire isn't some toy you can throw away when you're bored with it. People like us—people with power, with influence—don't just walk away. We don't quit. We don't leave behind everything we've built just to play house in some backwater town."

Julian clenched his fists at his sides, a deep, guttural frustration rising within him. He had spent his life hiding behind the shadows of his father's success. He had always known the price of his family's empire—the price of the power and wealth that came with it. But now, standing on the precipice of it all, he realized the cost was greater than he could have ever imagined. And yet, in this moment, he felt something stir inside him—

something raw and real.

He wasn't the same man he had been when he walked into this room. The man who was willing to walk away from everything was different. And he wouldn't let Richard, or his father, strip that away from him.

"You're wrong, Richard," Julian said, the words coming faster now. "I'm not afraid of losing your empire. I'm not afraid of you. But you know what I'm afraid of? Living the rest of my life in a cage. A cage built by my father's empire. A cage that's meant to keep me in line. I'm done with it. I'm done with living for someone else."

Richard stepped closer, the gun still pressed against Julian's temple. "You think you can just walk away from this?" he repeated, his voice seething with contempt. "You think you have the luxury of choosing a different path? Your father will never let you go, Julian. Not like this."

A cold wave of realization washed over Julian. Richard was right in one way. His father's influence was far-reaching, and no matter how much Julian tried to escape it, no matter how far he ran, there would always be a pull. But that didn't mean Julian had to bend to it. He had made his choice. And now, it was time to prove that he wasn't afraid to stand by it.

He met Richard's eyes, steady and unflinching. "Maybe I don't need to run anymore," Julian said, his voice low but firm. "Maybe it's time for me to face my father—face him on my own terms."

For a long moment, Richard didn't speak, and Julian wondered if he had said the wrong thing. The tension in the air was thick, suffocating, as though they were both waiting for something—waiting for the other to make a move, to break the stalemate. But the silence was broken by a voice from behind.

"You're right."

Julian turned, startled, his pulse quickening as he saw Greg step out from the shadows. His heart sank as he saw the familiar figure, his mind immediately racing to make sense of the situation. Greg had always been loyal to him. He had always been the one person who had stood by his side, who had been there when Julian needed him the most. But now, standing there, Greg's face was cold—empty of the warmth Julian had once relied on.

"What the hell is going on, Greg?" Julian demanded, his voice tight with confusion and fear. "Why are you here?"

Greg didn't answer immediately. Instead, he walked forward, his gaze flickering between Julian and Richard. Finally, he spoke, his voice low and calm. "Because this was never about you, Julian. It was never about the empire, the power, the wealth. This was always about control."

Julian's mind raced. "Control? What are you talking about?"

Greg's eyes flickered toward Richard, and then back to Julian. "You've been a pawn in your father's game for a long time, Julian. I've been a pawn, too. But this isn't about the business anymore.

It's about something much bigger. And it's time for you to finally understand that."

Julian's heart began to pound in his chest as the pieces began to fall into place. "You..." He couldn't finish the sentence. The realization hit him like a ton of bricks. His loyalty to Greg, the trust he had placed in him, had been misplaced. Greg had never been on his side. He had been playing a part all along.

"I didn't want it to be like this," Greg continued, his voice flat, unemotional. "But your father's orders were clear. We can't let you walk away. Not after everything he's built."

Julian's pulse raced. His mind spun with the implications of Greg's words. The life he had tried to build with Clara, the future he had dreamed of—all of it was slipping through his fingers. His father had already planned this. He had orchestrated everything from the beginning, manipulating everyone around him, including Greg, to ensure that Julian would return to the fold.

"You've been working for him all along, haven't you?" Julian's voice was barely a whisper, the weight of the betrayal settling deep within him.

Greg didn't flinch. "It was never about you, Julian. It was about the bigger picture. Your father doesn't take kindly to those who defy him. And now you've defied him. And now, you'll pay the price."

Julian's heart sank. "You'll kill me, won't you?" he asked, his voice trembling despite his best efforts to stay composed.

Richard chuckled, the sound dark and cold. "Not kill you, Julian. But you'll wish we had. This isn't just about business. This is about control. And you've just made the biggest mistake of your life."

Before Julian could react, Greg made a swift movement. The cold metal of a cuff clicked around Julian's wrist, and before he could even try to pull away, he felt the sharp tug of his own body being pulled back against the wall. He was trapped. No matter what he did, no matter how much he fought, he was caught in the web of lies, betrayal, and family that had haunted him for so long.

Greg looked at him one last time, the emotion in his eyes unreadable. "You made your choice, Julian. Now it's time to face the consequences."

Julian's breath hitched as the realization hit him. There was no escaping it. His father's empire, his life—everything he had fought so hard to leave behind—was about to swallow him whole.

And the only way out, he realized, was to make a choice he hadn't been prepared for. A choice that would cost him everything he thought he wanted.

"Clara..." he whispered, the name a prayer, a plea for the one thing he still held on to.

Thirteen

Rebuilding the Bridge

The cold morning mist clung to the streets of the small town, wrapping around the buildings and weaving through the trees like the remnants of a dream that had faded with the rising sun. Julian stood at the edge of the park, his hands stuffed into the pockets of his jacket, his breath forming clouds in the crisp air. It was early, too early for most of the town to be awake, and yet here he was, waiting. Waiting for something, or someone. He wasn't sure which.

The past few days had been a blur—an endless cycle of meetings, phone calls, and strained conversations with Greg. The web of lies and betrayal had tangled itself around him tighter than ever before. His father's threats had been more than just words. They had been the reality he had been trying to escape. He had thought he could walk away, start over with Clara, build something real. But the truth was, his past wasn't so easily discarded. His father's empire had a hold on him that went deeper than he had realized.

But now, after everything—after the gun, the betrayal, the pain—there was one thing that had kept him going: Clara. She had given him a chance, a glimmer of hope, and in the midst of all the chaos, he realized that he couldn't lose that. He couldn't lose her.

He had made his choice. He would fight for it. But how?

Julian pulled out his phone and checked the time again. It had been hours since he had sent her the message. Since he had written down the words, the ones that felt impossible, but necessary.

Clara, I know I don't deserve your forgiveness, but I can't let this end like it did. Please, let me explain. Please let me prove to you that I'm not the man I was before. That I'm ready to be the man you deserve. I'm ready to fight for you. If you'll let me.

His thumb hovered over the screen for a moment, debating whether or not to send it again. He didn't want to pressure her. He didn't want to seem desperate. But the truth was, he was desperate. Desperate for another chance. Desperate to fix what he had broken.

Just as he was about to put the phone away, it buzzed in his hand. The name on the screen made his heart skip a beat.

Clara.

He quickly answered, his breath catching in his throat. “Clara?”

“Julian.” Her voice came through, soft but steady. “I got your message.”

Julian’s heart raced as he took a step back, his mind spinning. He had no idea what to say, what to expect. His emotions were a storm inside him—hope, fear, uncertainty, all tangled together.

“Clara, I—” He stopped, swallowing hard. “I’m so sorry for everything. For the lies. For making you doubt me. I never wanted to hurt you. You mean everything to me.”

There was a long pause on the other end, and Julian’s stomach twisted with the uncertainty of what was coming. Would she hang up? Would she tell him it was too late?

Finally, Clara spoke again, her voice quieter this time. “I need you to understand something, Julian. What you did… it hurt. It hurt more than you’ll ever know. I don’t know if I can just forget what happened. But I also know that I can’t keep carrying around this weight of anger and resentment. I need to understand that you’re not the man who lied to me. The man who used me.”

Julian’s chest tightened. He had known this would be a test. But hearing it from her, hearing the pain in her voice, made the reality of what he had done crash down on him harder than anything else. “Clara, I’m not that man,” he said, his voice steady despite the turmoil inside. “I can’t undo the past, but I can show you that I’m not the man who hurt you. I want to prove it to you.

I'm willing to do whatever it takes. Just give me the chance."

There was a long pause, and Julian held his breath, waiting. He could hear the faint sound of Clara's breath on the other end of the line, the silence stretching between them like an ocean that neither of them knew how to cross.

Finally, Clara spoke again, her voice softer, almost hesitant. "I'm willing to listen, Julian. But you have to show me. You can't just tell me things are different. You have to show me."

Relief washed over him in waves, but it was tempered by the realization of just how much work lay ahead of him. He wasn't sure how he was going to prove it to her, how he was going to rebuild the trust he had shattered. But he knew one thing for sure: he wouldn't give up. Not now. Not when Clara was the one thing he had left to fight for.

"I'll show you, Clara," he said, his voice thick with emotion. "I'll show you every day for as long as it takes."

—-

The following days were a blur of effort, small moments, and hard work. Julian knew he couldn't erase the past in an instant. He couldn't undo the lies he had told, the mistakes he had made. But he could start to rebuild. Slowly. Methodically.

He knew that regaining Clara's trust wouldn't be easy. But it had to start somewhere. He began by focusing on the small things—the things that might seem insignificant to someone else, but meant the world to Clara. He picked up a canvas and started painting again, something he had done in his youth, something he had abandoned in favor of his father's business. He couldn't remember the last time he had felt free enough to pick up a brush, but with each stroke, he felt himself coming alive again. It was a small act, but one that spoke volumes to him about the life he wanted.

And each evening, when the sun dipped below the horizon and the sky was streaked with shades of orange and pink, he would find Clara at the café. They would sit together in silence for a while, a comfortable quiet that Julian had come to appreciate. He didn't try to force anything. He didn't try to fill the silence with words. Instead, he allowed it to linger, understanding that healing wasn't a quick process. It took time.

At first, Clara was reserved, her eyes wary when she looked at him, her smile tight. But with every passing day, something changed. A small spark of warmth returned. She began to open up again, just a little, allowing him glimpses of the woman he had fallen in love with. They spoke about everything—about art, about the world beyond the small town, about the dreams they had tucked away.

And then, one evening, after several days of quiet companionship, Clara turned to him as they sat at the café. She looked into his eyes, her expression serious, but softened by something that made Julian's chest tighten with hope.

"You've been trying," Clara said, her voice steady, but there was something in her gaze that made Julian's heart skip. "And I can see it. I can see that you're not the man you were before. I still don't know if I can trust you completely. But… I'm willing to try. I'm willing to rebuild this."

Julian felt as if the ground beneath him had shifted. For the first time in a long time, he allowed himself to feel the faintest stir of hope. The bridge was still fragile. But they were starting to rebuild it, step by step.

He reached for her hand, his touch tentative at first, but when Clara didn't pull away, he let his fingers curl around hers. "I won't stop trying, Clara," he said, his voice thick with emotion. "I won't stop proving to you that I'm not the man I was. Not the man who hid from everything. I'll do whatever it takes."

Clara smiled softly, the expression genuine but still cautious. "I know you will. And that's what scares me the most," she said, her voice low. "Because now, I'm afraid that if I let you back in completely, I'll lose myself in you again."

Julian squeezed her hand gently, his eyes locking with hers. "I'm not asking you to lose yourself. I'm asking you to trust that I won't ask you to. That we can build something together, something real."

For a moment, there was only silence between them. The world outside continued to move, oblivious to the small shift that was happening at this table, this quiet moment in time. But inside Julian, something had changed. The weight of the past hadn't disappeared, but it no longer held him prisoner.

Clara looked at him, and this time, when she smiled, it was real. It was soft, tender, and full of something Julian hadn't felt in a long time: hope.

"I'm willing to try," she said again, her voice firm but warm. "But this time, we'll do it on our terms. Together."

And in that moment, Julian knew that this—whatever this was, whatever came next—would be the true test. But it wasn't just about him anymore. It was about them, together. And for the first time in his life, Julian felt like he was finally ready to face whatever came next. Not as the man his father had shaped, not as the man who had hidden behind his wealth, but as the man who had chosen to rebuild a bridge from the ground up, piece by piece, until it was strong enough to carry both of them.

Fourteen

A Leap of Faith

The moon hung high in the sky, its light a pale beacon amidst the darkness that cloaked the town. Julian stood at the edge of the small park, staring out into the quiet night. The crisp air wrapped around him like a second skin, and for the first time in what felt like ages, he could breathe. The weight of the world, the crushing expectations that had always followed him, seemed to lift, if only for a moment. But in that moment, the questions that had been plaguing him for days—weeks, even—seemed to fade into the background. The questions that had kept him up at night, questioning his every move, every decision, all seemed irrelevant now.

Because the one thing he had feared the most, the one thing that had haunted him for years, was finally staring him in the face: trust.

It was a simple word, one that everyone took for granted, but for Julian, trust had always been a foreign concept. His life had been built on a foundation of lies, deceit, and power. But now, standing here in the stillness of the night, he realized something. The foundation he had spent so long building, the one that had felt like the only thing he could rely on, was crumbling. And for the first time, he didn't feel afraid. He felt… free.

The sound of footsteps behind him broke his reverie, and Julian turned to see Clara approaching, her silhouette emerging from the shadows. She moved with purpose, her steps measured, yet there was something in her stride that suggested hesitation. A quiet uncertainty that mirrored his own.

Julian's breath caught in his chest. Every moment that had led to this—every conversation, every glance, every touch—had led them to this point. And yet, as Clara drew closer, he realized he still didn't know what would come next. He didn't know if the leap of faith he had taken was enough. He didn't know if they were ready. But one thing was certain: this moment would change everything.

Clara stopped a few paces away from him, her eyes searching his face, as though trying to read the unspoken words that hung between them. There was a quiet intensity in the air, an almost palpable tension that seemed to hum like electricity. Julian opened his mouth to speak, but the words caught in his throat. It was as though all the things he had been dying to say, all the apologies, all the promises, all the hopes for the future, had been swallowed up by the enormity of what they were both facing.

Finally, Clara spoke, her voice soft but steady. "I didn't come here to hear more apologies, Julian. I came because I need to know if you're really ready to let go of the past. I need to know if you're ready to let go of everything you've been hiding behind."

Her words were a challenge, a question, and yet, there was a vulnerability in her tone that struck Julian like a blow to the chest. He had spent so long hiding from the truth, from the person he had been, that now, facing Clara—facing the life he had wanted, the life he still wanted—he realized something.

"I'm not sure what the future holds," Julian said, his voice raw, his gaze fixed on Clara as he spoke. "But I know that I can't keep running. I can't keep hiding from who I am, from what I've done. I've spent too long trying to be someone I'm not. And maybe... maybe that's the reason I've never felt at peace."

Clara's eyes softened, but her gaze never wavered from his. "You don't have to be perfect, Julian. You don't have to have all the answers. But you do have to trust me. You have to trust that I'm here, that I'm willing to walk through this with you. But you have to take the leap. You have to trust yourself."

Julian's heart pounded in his chest, his breath coming faster now. She was right. He had spent so much time hiding, so much time pretending to be something he wasn't. But in this moment, he understood that the only way forward was to trust. Not just Clara, not just their relationship, but himself. For the first time, he felt the stirrings of something he had never truly believed in: hope.

He had spent so long chasing after power, after control, after approval. But what had it gotten him? An empty life, a fractured soul, a history full of mistakes. Clara had given him the chance to start over, to rebuild everything he had lost. And yet, he still hesitated. Fear was a silent companion, lurking just beyond the edge of his thoughts, reminding him of the consequences of failure. But Clara's words rang in his ears.

You have to trust yourself.

"I don't know what happens next," Julian said, his voice tight, but there was a clarity in his words now, something steady. "But I know I can't keep pretending. I can't keep hiding from who I am. I want this. I want you. But I can't ask you to be with someone who's still afraid of the past."

Clara stepped closer, her hand reaching out to him, her fingers brushing against his. Her touch was warm, grounding him in the moment, and for the first time in what felt like forever, Julian felt his walls come down. The fear, the uncertainty, all of it melted away as she stood there, offering him the one thing he had always longed for: acceptance.

"I'm scared too," Clara whispered, her voice barely audible in the quiet night. "But I'm not afraid of you. I'm afraid of what we could lose if we don't try. I'm afraid of letting the past keep us from building something real."

Her words were a revelation, a quiet truth that broke through the fog of Julian's thoughts. He didn't have to be perfect. He didn't have to have all the answers. He just had to trust. And, for the first time, he believed he could.

"I'm ready," Julian said, his voice full of conviction. "I'm ready to take the leap."

The words felt like a release, like he was finally letting go of everything that had kept him chained to the past. He reached for Clara, his hand trembling slightly as he cupped her face, pulling her closer. The moment felt timeless, like the world around them had stopped, holding its breath as they stood on the edge of something new.

Clara's lips met his, soft and tentative at first, but there was something in that kiss—something that spoke of the trust they were beginning to rebuild, of the leap they were taking together. It was as though the weight of all the years of lies, the fear, the uncertainty, had finally been lifted, replaced by the quiet certainty of what they were now.

When they pulled away, Clara smiled softly, her eyes reflecting a warmth that Julian hadn't seen in a long time. "You took the leap, Julian," she said quietly. "And I'm right here with you."

Julian's heart swelled in his chest, his breath coming in short bursts as he looked at her. It was a simple statement, but it carried the weight of everything they had been through, everything they had endured to get to this point. And in that moment, Julian knew that no matter what came next, they would face it together.

But just as he opened his mouth to speak again, the distant

sound of a car engine interrupted the moment. Julian's heart skipped a beat, the tension from the past few weeks rising again. It was a sound he knew all too well—the sound of his father's car.

Clara's eyes flickered toward the road, then back to Julian, a question in her gaze. He could feel the uncertainty creeping back in, the familiar sense of dread that had haunted him for so long. But this time, it didn't seem as overwhelming. This time, he was ready to face whatever came next.

"Do you think…" Clara started, her voice trailing off, her words hanging in the air.

"I don't know," Julian answered, his voice calm, his hand still resting gently against her cheek. "But whatever it is, I'm ready for it. I'm ready to face my father, to face everything I've been running from. And this time, I won't do it alone."

As the car grew louder, Julian took a deep breath, his heart steadying. Whatever happened next, whatever his father had in store, it didn't matter. The bridge between them was already rebuilt, and Julian had taken the leap of faith.

And this time, he was ready to soar.

Fifteen

True Love's Reward

The sound of tires crunching against gravel echoed in the quiet night as Julian stood at the edge of the park, his hands shoved deep into his coat pockets, his breath visible in the cool air. The wind had picked up again, howling through the trees as if urging him to face whatever was coming. Clara was beside him, her presence a quiet but powerful force that anchored him in this uncertain moment.

The car—his father's car—slowed as it neared the entrance to the park. Julian could feel his heart pounding in his chest, but his hands remained steady. This was it. This was the moment that would define everything.

He had spent the past few days preparing for this. Every word, every conversation, every plan—he had rehearsed them over and over in his mind. He had made the choice. He had walked away from his father's empire. He had chosen Clara, chosen the life he wanted for himself. But that didn't mean there weren't consequences. His father wouldn't let him go so easily.

The headlights of the car illuminated the path ahead, and Julian felt a familiar, suffocating weight settle over him. It was as if time itself had slowed, each second stretching into eternity. He knew his father's presence well—he had always been a force to be reckoned with, a man who demanded respect, whose gaze could freeze anyone in their tracks. But tonight, Julian wasn't afraid. Tonight, he would face the man who had shaped him, the man who had tried to control him for so long, and he would stand his ground.

Clara's hand slipped into his, and Julian looked at her, her face calm but with a glimmer of apprehension in her eyes. She had been his rock, the one person who had believed in him when even he had lost faith. Her touch reminded him of the choice he had made—of the love they shared. And in that moment, he knew that whatever happened next, it was worth it. He was worth it.

The car came to a stop, and the door swung open with a familiar, authoritative creak. Robert Hart, the man who had built an empire, stepped out, his tall, imposing figure casting a shadow over the night. His eyes were sharp, calculating, as they locked onto Julian. The years of tension, the weight of unspoken words, the broken expectations—all of it hung between them like an invisible wall.

Robert didn't speak immediately. He simply stood there,

assessing his son as if he were a pawn on a chessboard, waiting to decide his next move. His presence was overwhelming, suffocating, and for a moment, Julian felt that old fear creeping up again—the fear of being nothing more than an extension of the man who had raised him, the fear of disappointing him once more.

But Julian stood tall, his back straight, his chin lifted. He wasn't that man anymore. He wasn't the man who had hidden behind lies, behind wealth, behind expectations. He was Julian Hart, the man who had made a choice. And tonight, he would prove it.

"What are you doing here, Julian?" Robert's voice was cold, measured, but there was an edge to it that betrayed the fury simmering beneath the surface.

"I'm here to talk," Julian said, his voice steady, firm. He didn't flinch. He couldn't afford to. "I've made my choice, and I'm not going back."

Robert's eyes narrowed, the muscles in his jaw tightening as if the words were a personal insult. He took a step forward, his movements deliberate. "You think you can just walk away from everything? From me? From your future?" His voice was low, filled with a cold, cutting anger. "I built this empire for you, Julian. For you. And this is how you repay me?"

Julian felt Clara's presence beside him, the warmth of her hand in his a silent reminder of everything he had fought for. He glanced at her, and she gave him a small, reassuring smile—one that reminded him of how far they had come. He turned his attention back to his father, his resolve hardening. He was no longer that boy who had feared his father's wrath. He was a man now, and he would face whatever came next with the strength he had fought so hard to find.

"I'm not walking away from you, Father," Julian said, his voice steady. "I'm walking away from the life you chose for me. I'm choosing to live my own life. To make my own choices. You can't control me anymore."

Robert's eyes flickered with disbelief. He took another step forward, his voice rising now, his tone cold and commanding. "You think you can just walk away from everything I've built? From the legacy? From the power? You think you'll just be happy with her?" He gestured to Clara, his words dripping with disdain. "She's nothing but a distraction, Julian. You're throwing away everything I've given you for a woman who doesn't understand the world you come from. A woman who could never give you what I can."

Julian's chest tightened at the venom in his father's words, but he didn't back down. This was the man who had spent his life telling Julian that nothing mattered except success. The man who had taught him to hide his true self behind a mask of power. But Julian had learned, over the past few months, that real success wasn't in money or power. It was in the choices you made, in the people you loved, in the courage to be vulnerable. And Clara had shown him that.

"She understands me, Father," Julian said, his voice unwavering.

"She's the only one who has. And that's why I'm with her. Because she sees me for who I truly am, not for the man you wanted me to be."

Robert's face twisted in a sneer. "You think she's going to save you? You think love is going to solve all your problems? You're a fool, Julian. A fool who's going to regret this decision for the rest of his life."

The words hit Julian like a punch to the gut, but he refused to let them break him. He wasn't the boy who had been afraid of his father's wrath anymore. He wasn't afraid of regret. He had already made his choice, and he would stand by it.

"I'm not afraid of regret," Julian said, his voice low but firm. "I'm not afraid of losing the life you built for me. I'm not afraid of losing anything anymore. Because I've found something that matters more than all of this. I've found a love that's real. I've found the courage to be myself."

There was a long, tense silence between them. Robert stood there, glaring at his son, his expression hard and unforgiving. For a moment, Julian wondered if his father would strike him, if he would try to force him back into his world with threats or violence. But the moment passed, and instead of anger, there was something else in Robert's eyes—a flicker of realization. A flicker of defeat.

"You've made your choice, Julian," Robert said quietly, his voice cold and emotionless. "But don't think this is over. You'll regret this. You'll come crawling back. You'll see. This isn't a life you can just walk away from."

Julian met his father's gaze, his chest tight with the weight of everything they had just shared. There was no fear left in him—not of Robert, not of the life that awaited him, not of the consequences. He had made his choice. And he would live with it, whatever came next.

"No, Father," Julian said, his voice steady and final. "This is the life I've chosen. And I won't regret it. Not ever."

For a moment, Robert stood there, his eyes searching Julian's face, as if looking for a crack, a sign of weakness, something that would convince him to take it all back. But Julian didn't flinch. He stood his ground, unwavering.

Robert's gaze shifted to Clara, and for the first time, Julian saw something in his father's eyes that he hadn't seen before. It wasn't anger. It wasn't fear. It was a quiet understanding. A recognition of something Julian had never fully understood until this moment: that his son was no longer his to control.

With a final, almost imperceptible nod, Robert turned and walked back to his car. He didn't say another word, didn't look back, and within moments, the engine roared to life, the sound of the tires peeling away into the night.

Julian stood there, his heart still pounding in his chest, but something in him had shifted. Something had changed. He had stood up to the man who had ruled his life for so long. And in doing so, he had taken his first true step into the future.

Clara's hand slipped into his, and for the first time in a long time, Julian felt the weight of the world lift from his shoulders. They stood there, together, in the quiet of the night, knowing that the road ahead wouldn't be easy. There would be challenges, there would be sacrifices. But in that moment, they both understood something that nothing could take away: they had each other. And that was enough.

"Are you okay?" Clara asked softly, her voice full of concern as she looked up at him.

Julian smiled, a smile that felt real for the first time in a long time. "I'm more than okay. I'm free."

And in that moment, Julian realized that the reward of true love wasn't in the easy choices or the perfect moments. It was in the courage to make the hard choices, to fight for what mattered, and to trust that, no matter what came next, they would face it together.